Digital Inheritance

Strategies for Safeguarding Crypto Assets and Blockchain Information

Table of Contents

Chapter 1. Introduction

As more individuals venture into the exciting universe of cryptocurrencies and blockchain, one previously overlooked aspect has started to gain importance: Digital Inheritance. In this Special Report, we explore the phenomenon of Digital Inheritance and analyze strategies to safeguard crypto-assets and blockchain information after the owner's passing. Whether you're a seasoned crypto investor or a novice, the necessity of planning for your digital assets' future can't be overstated. It doesn't require an expert to understand the importance; even if the discussions around crypto are often technical, the idea behind digital inheritance is straightforward and involves everybody. Adopt a proactive approach and secure not just your physical wealth, but also your digital legacy, because even in the afterlife, every Satoshi counts. Get ready to deepen your crypto-knowledge too by decoding blockchain information safety. Gain insights which you can apply personally or professionally; either way, this report promises value at every turn.

Chapter 2. Understanding Digital Inheritance: An Overview

Asset management has long been a cornerstone of financial planning. In recent years, the advent of cryptocurrencies and blockchain technologies has broadened the scope of assets to include digital assets. Digital Inheritance refers to the thought-out anticipation, planning, and facilitation processes that ensure your digital assets are efficiently passed to your chosen individuals upon your demise. Whether you own Bitcoin, Ether, or digital art, it's crucial to consider what happens with these when you are no longer around.

2.1. Crypto Assets as Inheritable Property

Traditionally, inheritance has involved assets such as real estate, bank deposits, stocks, and other material goods. In the eyes of law and society, these are tangible assets that could be passed down from generation to generation. However, the explosion of cryptocurrencies and blockchain technology has introduced a new class of assets: Digital Assets.

Digital assets are assets stored on digital platforms. These include cryptocurrencies like Bitcoin, Ethereum, and many others, digital tokens, digital contracts, and more. These assets are governed by cryptographic security and are stored on blockchains - decentralized databases that securely store information across thousands or even millions of computers. This decentralization and cryptographic security make these assets extremely secure, but also challenging to recover or transfer without the necessary information or codes, noticeably if the owner is no longer alive.

Many early adopters of technology or cryptocurrencies who have amassed substantial digital wealth face the problem that in the event of sudden death, their digital fortune could be lost forever. Technically, upon the death of a cryptocurrency owner, the ownership of the coins is transferred to whoever can access them using private keys, akin to finding a buried treasure without a map if you're not prepared beforehand.

2.2. Planning for Digital Assets

Estate planning for digital assets is a somewhat murky area as it's relatively new and varies significantly from traditional asset planning. Unlike a traditional bank or investment account, digital assets typically aren't held with a custodian who can facilitate the transfer of wealth upon death. Instead, digital assets are often stored in digital wallets or exchanges that require keys or passwords that only the owner might know. If these passcodes are lost, the assets can be incredibly difficult or even impossible to recover.

Despite the challenges, planning for digital assets shouldn't be overlooked because of their potential value. A well-implemented digital inheritance plan includes a comprehensive list of your digital assets, the storage locations of these assets, and a secure mechanism to transfer passwords, keys, or relevant access information to your intended beneficiaries.

2.3. Legal Aspects of Digital Inheritance

Legal aspects of digital inheritance can prove to be another field fraught with complication. Varying laws worldwide mean that legal status and treatment of digital assets differ enormously from one jurisidiction to another. In the absence of a clearly defined legal framework for digital assets, it is advisable to consult with an attorney experienced in estate planning for digital assets.

Cross-border inheritance can further complicate matters, given the global nature of cryptocurrencies. As a result, it's crucial to keep ongoing changes to international law and policy regarding digital assets monitored and understood.

2.4. User Mortality and Blockchain Technology

Blockchain technology itself adds another layer of complexity. Designed to provide security and anonymity to users, blockchain technology does not have a centralized authority that can override a user's private key or recover lost keys. This means that without your private key, your digital assets become inaccessible, even to your heirs.

This has led to the phenomenon of "zombie coins," digital assets belonging to deceased owners that are forever locked away because of lost private keys. Proactively planning how your keys will be passed on can prevent your digital assets from becoming another zombie coin statistic.

2.5. Tools and Techniques for Digital Inheritance

Various methods and platforms can facilitate the transition of digital assets. These include legacy platforms specifically designed to safeguard your digital assets and provide a means of passing on critical information to your heirs. Dead man's switches, multisignature wallets, and smart contracts are other tools used to ensure that digital assets are not lost.

Various third-party services also offer digital inheritance tools and solutions. However, these services often come with their own sets of challenges, including security concerns and the need for regular updating of access codes and keys.

In conclusion, managing digital inheritance is an essential aspect of being a responsible digital asset owner. With no universal solution to this issue yet, it's vital to keep abreast of tools, best practices, and laws regarding cryptocurrencies and digital inheritance. Which makes this a challenging but equally crucial chore, as we navigate the legacy of wealth in the digital age.

Chapter 3. Comprehending Cryptocurrencies and Blockchain Technology

Before drowning into the depths of the technicalities and intricacies of Digital Inheritance, understanding the nuts and bolts of Cryptocurrencies and Blockchain technology is crucial. Precisely, the more you comprehend cryptocurrencies and blockchain, the better you'd be at managing and safeguarding these digital assets.

3.1. The Advent of Cryptocurrencies

In 2009, cryptocurrencies made a spectacular debut with the introduction of Bitcoin, the first decentralized digital currency powered by blockchain technology. It was invented by an unknown person or group of people using the pseudonym Satoshi Nakamoto. The main idea was to create a medium of exchange that does not require a centralized authority, is digitally secure and allows peer-to-peer transactions.

Since then, the crypto space has expanded dramatically with over 5000 different types of cryptocurrencies as of 2021. Ethereum, Ripple, Litecoin, and Bitcoin Cash are just a few among many digital currencies. These digital assets are created by complex computational procedures known as mining, and their transactions are made on respective blockchain networks.

3.2. Understanding Blockchain Technology

Blockchain can be envisioned as a digital ledger of transactions distributed across a network of computer systems. Each block contains a number of transactions, and whenever a new transaction occurs on this blockchain, a record is added to every participant's ledger.

The decentralized nature of the block means that no single authority has control over the information. This not only addresses the issue of a single point of failure but also makes it difficult for the data to be manipulated or changed by unauthorized entities.

Blockchain technology, the backbone of cryptocurrencies, offers some considerable advantages such as:

- Control and security: Blockchain technology allows users to control their money, rather than relying on banks or governments. The public and private keys associated with cryptocurrencies safeguard the transactions.

- Speed and efficacy: A blockchain transaction can be quicker and more efficient than a traditional financial mechanism.

- Transparency: While maintaining the confidentiality of the users, the blockchain exhibits a transparent transaction history.

3.3. Cryptography in Cryptocurrencies and Blockchain

Exchange of cryptocurrencies involves a method known as cryptography. Cryptography is the process of encoding and decoding information to ensure secure communication. In the realm of cryptocurrencies, it is used to securely record transactions on the blockchain. Each transaction is encrypted with an algorithm that makes the details hidden and secure.

A pair of keys, a public key and a private key, is used in the cryptographic transactions. Everyone in the network can see the public key, which is like your email address, while the private key is known only to the wallet owner. It is imperative to securely store your private keys, as anyone who has access to this key can control the funds associated with the public key.

3.4. Wallets and Exchanges

Cryptocurrency wallets and exchanges are essential components in handling cryptocurrencies. A digital wallet is used to store, send, and receive cryptocurrencies. They are secured by cryptographic methods, where each wallet has a pair of keys- the private key and the public key.

Exchanges, on the other hand, are platforms that facilitate buying, selling, and trading cryptocurrencies. It is worth noting that a number of exchanges have fallen victim to security breaches in the past, leading to substantial losses. Therefore, choosing a secure exchange and using additional security measures such as two-factor authentication (2FA) is important.

3.5. The Volatile Nature of Cryptocurrencies

Cryptocurrencies are noted for their volatile nature. The prices can fluctuate dramatically over short periods due to various factors. Supply and demand, market sentiment, political events, technological developments, and regulatory news can all significantly influence the value of cryptocurrencies. Therefore, while they can provide substantial returns, they also pose risks.

3.6. Mining and Proof of Work

Mining refers to the process of validating new transactions and recording them on the global ledger (blockchain). Cryptocurrency mining involves two key functions: releasing new cryptocurrency into the system, and verifying and adding transactions to the blockchain.

Proof of Work (PoW) is a consensus algorithm used in blockchain to confirm transactions and produce new blocks. The central principle behind PoW is to solve a complex mathematical problem which is hard to compute but easy to verify.

While cryptocurrencies and blockchain technology bring a new paradigm to our financial system, understanding their intricacies is critical for their effective use and management. Essentially, existing within the digital sphere, it is through understanding that one can ensure the safety of these assets, which in turn, leads to the importance of digital inheritance in the entire blockchain sphere. The following chapters will focus on this very concept and provide guidelines to secure your digital inheritance effectively.

Chapter 4. The Need for Safeguarding Crypto Assets: A New Reality

For many individuals, venturing into the realm of cryptocurrency can be an exciting exploration of new possibilities. However, it's vitally important to make a conscious effort to safeguard these assets, like any other part of your financial repertoire.

4.1. The Evolution of Wealth

With the evolution of technology, the way we perceive wealth has changed significantly. We now have digital assets alongside physical ones. Cryptocurrencies, NFTs, and other digital assets have paved a new way for wealth accumulation. But this digital expansion also requires an updated and complex security system, replacing the conventional safety deposit boxes and home safes for these intangible assets.

4.2. The Risk Factor

The technology tied to cryptocurrencies and digital assets presents an array of new risk factors. The private keys required to access these digital wealth troves act as a double-edged sword. Whilst providing a robust level of security, they also pose a risk if misplaced or forgotten. Catastrophes occur when these keys fall into the wrong hands or cannot be retrieved upon the owner's demise, leading to permanent loss of assets.

In addition to this, the operating pattern of blockchain itself harbors risks. Since the technology works on decentralized ledger systems, there are no central authorities or institutions that can help retrieve lost assets.

4.3. The Role of Digital Inheritance

Herein lies the importance of digital inheritance, a provision to ensure your wealth doesn't turn inaccessible or is lost after your lifetime. Like a will or legacy, digital inheritance comes as a 'Will 2.0,' keeping the spirit of the old system but modernizing it to incorporate the digital future.

4.4. Traditional Estate Planning vs Digital Inheritance

Traditional estate planning has always been an integral part of wealth management. However, it falls short when it comes to handling digital assets. As more individuals accumulate considerable sums in digital currencies, there's an increasing need to incorporate these assets in estate planning.

Digital inheritance planning differs in that it isn't enough to just **mention** your digital assets and then transfer ownership. It requires the careful exchange of private keys, passwords, and other security measures such that the heir can access the wealth securely without causing potential security vulnerabilities.

4.5. Implementing a Digital Inheritance Plan

Accomplishing a digital inheritance plan is two-fold; it involves a succession plan for your digital assets, as well as ensuring your secrets to access those assets are shared safely.

1. Identify all your digital assets: From cryptocurrency to digital

wallets, online trading accounts, social media assets, and virtual property, make a complete list.

2. Determine their value: Depending upon the volatility and market factors, evaluate their worth.

3. Decide beneficiaries: Assign each digital asset to a beneficiary. If you have multiple people in mind, it might be practical to organize the assets proportionately.

4. Document access method: Provide a secure process for your benefactors to retrieve these assets. This might mean sharing a private key or access to a digital wallet.

5. Review and update: As with any form of planning, this step repeats itself over time. As you acquire new digital assets or as the benefits change, it's crucial to revisit your plan.

4.6. Use of Third-Party Services

To further streamline the process and maintain security, entrepreneurs and blockchain firms have started offering digital inheritance services. These organizations operate on various models, including smart contracts triggered by specific events (like death), multi-signature wallets requiring more than one person's 'signature' to execute a transaction, or even technological solutions combining AI with blockchain technology.

4.7. Legal Considerations

Despite the headway in technologies facilitating digital asset inheritance, the legal landscape isn't as advanced. As a result, laws pertaining to digital assets and their succession are absent or embryonic at best in most jurisdictions.

As solutions become more mainstream, it's anticipated that legal provisions will evolve to incorporate digital inheritance, offering protection and structure to those passing on digital assets. Till that happens, it's up to individual owners to ensure they have adequate measures in place to secure their digital legacy.

4.8. Wrap Up

Securing digital assets is no longer a mere afterthought. It's a necessity in the contemporary period where digital wealth is rapidly burgeoning. Cryptocurrency and digital inheritance are interlinked domains that can't be viewed in isolation. The urgency to safeguard these assets brings us face-to-face with the exciting, yet daunting, world of digital wealth management. In lieu of this, adopting digital inheritance strategies is not just prudent. It's essential.

Chapter 5. Tools and Solutions for Digital Asset Protection

Every day, the digital universe is expanding exponentially, and whether we realize it or not, at the forefront of this expansion are cryptocurrencies and blockchain technology. Guarding these digital assets, especially after our passing, is an aspect that requires immense attention. Therefore, it is crucial to explore the tools and solutions in place to protect these assets.

5.1. Hardware Wallets

Hardware wallets are a type of physical device where a user can store their private keys, a critical piece of information required to access and manage their blockchain assets. The essence of a hardware wallet is that it offers the convenience of saving digital assets offline, considerably reducing the likelihood of cyber theft. It's very much akin to a physical safe but in a digital platform.

One of the most favored hardware wallets by crypto users worldwide is Ledger. It offers a wallet apps like Ledger Live, which lets you manage your assets from your computer. Also, its security implementation such as PIN code and two-factor authentication adds to the safety of the stored crypto-assets.

The alternative to Ledger is the Trezor Wallet, offering similar features, safety, and security for your digital assets.

5.2. Software Wallets

Unlike hardware wallets that come as physical devices, software wallets are just applications or software that can be installed on a computer or smartphone. While they offer a convenient way to handle crypto transactions, it's worth noting that they can be compromised if the system they are installed on is hacked. Software wallets are ideal for small amounts of cryptocurrencies which are actively traded or transacted.

Examples of software wallets are Exodus and Edge. These offer the ease of use, backup, and recovery features which are a necessity in the unpredictable world of cryptocurrencies.

5.3. Custodial Services

For individuals or organizations that have a significantly large amount of crypto-assets, custodial services can be a smart choice. Companies providing crypto custodial services manage the storage and security of cryptographic keys on behalf of their clients.

Gemini Custody and Coinbase Custody are two well-known custodial services in the crypto-world. Robust security measure, often to the extent of cold storage (offline storage of cryptocurrencies), is a common feature of these services.

5.4. Multi-signature Wallets

A significant advancement in digital asset protection is the concept of Multi-signature wallets. Essentially, these wallets require multiple private keys for a transaction to be processed. The required number of keys can be customized based on the user's preference. This adds another layer of security and can be a preventive measure for unauthorized transactions even in the event of a single key compromise.

BitGo and Electrum are two popular multi-signature wallet providers. While BitGo offers services particularly for businesses,

Electrum is more geared towards individual usage but does provide support for multi-signature wallets.

5.5. Inheritance Services

One of the critical considerations while discussing digital asset protection is the transition of these assets after the owner's demise. Failing to address this point might lead to a perpetual loss of the assets. Several crypto platforms and services provide solutions to avoid this scenario.

Safe Haven's inheritance solution, for example, offers a platform where the user can detail how their digital assets should be distributed or managed after their passing. Similar services are provided by Casa's Keymaster and TrustVerse, solving critical inheritance related issues in the digital world.

In conclusion, digital asset protection is a multi-faceted challenge that requires a comprehensive and foresighted approach. Tools and services, ranging from hardware and software wallets, custodial services, multi-signature wallets, and inheritance services are integral components for ensuring complete protection of one's digital assets. As we navigate the budding realm of cryptocurrencies and blockchain technology, it's crucial to continually update our strategies and stay abreast of advancements in digital asset protection. Doing so guarantees that our digital legacy is as secure and robust as our physical one.

Chapter 6. Smart Contracts in Estate Planning: Unlocking Potential

The innovative nature of blockchain technology has offered an intriguing aspect to estate planning, which was traditionally only associated with physical assets. Today, smart contracts are transforming the world of estate planning, providing not only security and automation but also ease of use in managing your digital assets.

6.1. The Essence of Smart Contracts

Smart contracts are self-executing contracts with the terms of the agreement between buyer and seller being directly written into lines of code. The code, and the agreements contained therein, exist across a distributed, decentralized blockchain network. Simply put, your smart contract is a computer program that automatically executes, controls, or documents legally relevant events and actions according to terms of an agreement, like a standard contract. The main difference here is the elimination of a third party, as the contract is built into the code.

The purpose of smart contracts is to provide security superior to traditional contract laws and to lower the transaction costs associated with contracting. Theoretically, they can be used in any context that traditional contracts are used, including in wills and estate planning.

6.2. Smart Contracts for Digital Assets

In the cryptocurrency world, a digital asset is any asset stored in a computer-readable binary format, accessible through a digital network—your cryptocurrencies or tokens are examples of such digital assets. As these assets are not physical, their handling, transfer, and inheritance take place digitally. Smart contracts have found a useful place in this field due to their transparent, immutable, and decentralized nature.

The most significant advantage is the ability to automate the process of inheritance. By using a smart contract, you can set the event of your death as a condition for the transfer of your assets. When this condition is met, your specified recipients will receive the digital assets without the need for a third-party executor.

6.3. Writing a Smart Contract for Digital Inheritance

Writing a smart contract for your digital inheritance starts with determining which digital assets you wish to include. This could range from a simple list of cryptocurrencies to including access to digital services and subscriptions.

Choose a platform or blockchain where you want your smart contract to live. Ethereum is the most popular for creating smart contracts because of its inherent support for programming languages. However, other blockchains like Binance Smart Chain, Solana, Polkadot, and others may also be viable choices depending on your preferences and requirements.

The next step is to choose a triggering event. In the case of digital inheritance, it may be a proof of death, verified through a reliable source. Ensure this aspect is considered carefully, as it needs to be a reliable automated trigger. Handling trigger event incorrectly may result in unexpected execution or non-execution of the contract.

Design the transfer mechanism. This usually involves deciding how your assets will be divided among your heirs and the method of transfer. It's much like designating beneficiaries and assigning them proportions of your estate. This part of the process will differ based on the specific capabilities and limitations of the blockchain where your smart contract resides.

After the initial design, writing the contract requires programming skills, specifically in the language supported by the chosen blockchain. If you are not a programmer, hiring a skilled blockchain developer might be necessary.

6.4. Legal Considerities and Challenges

Despite the clear potential, there are some legal challenges that you may run into. Smart contracts, and blockchain overall, are new developments. Legal systems around the world are still trying to catch up, and the legal status of smart contracts differs from jurisdiction to jurisdiction.

It's currently unclear whether wills written as smart contracts, where the contract itself stipulates the distribution of the decedent's assets, will be valid and enforceable. Furthermore, the anonymity associated with blockchain could make it difficult to verify the identity of heirs.

Also consider the security risks. Despite blockchain's security features, the code of your smart contract could be exploited if there's a loophole. Make sure to have your contract's code audited by security professionals.

6.5. The Future of Estate Planning with Smart Contracts

Smart contracts have significant potential to revolutionize estate planning. As the landscape of both digital assets and blockchain technology continue to evolve, the utility of smart contracts will likely become more appealing and diversified.

However, as with any new technology, the path forward is filled with both opportunities and challenges. Navigating these paths will require further technological advancements as well as legal and regulatory adaption and clarification.

It is no longer a question of whether digital assets can be a part of your legacy but rather how you want to plan for them. As we continue to move towards a digital society, it is increasingly apparent that estate planning needs to involve elements like smart contracts to make sure your digital legacy is protected and passed on according to your wishes. This crystalizes the importance of understanding smart contracts in estate planning, unlocking the potential of technology to protect and manage our digital assets after our departure.

Chapter 7. Blockchain Information Security: Essential Measures

Blockchain technology forms an essential pillar of digital inheritance, in particular cryptocurrency assets. However, much like any digital asset, the safety and security of these assets are paramount. In this analysis, we delve into critical measures you can take to ensure the security of blockchain information.

7.1. Understanding Blockchain Security

First, a proper understanding of blockchain security is necessary. A blockchain is a form of distributed ledger technology that records transactions across several devices, known as nodes. Essentially, a blockchain is an ever-growing chain of records, or blocks, that are linked using cryptography. Each block contains a cryptographic hash of the previous block, transaction data, and a timestamp.

The decentralized nature of a blockchain provides inherent security features as every transaction is transparent and tamper-evident - data once written into a block cannot be changed without changing all subsequent blocks and gaining the consensus of the network. This makes the blockchain technology resistant to modification, ensuring data integrity and authenticity.

However, despite its security features, blockchain technology isn't absolute in its vulnerability. Factors such as user error, sophisticated hacking attempts, and the vulnerability of connected systems can compromise blockchain's security.

7.2. Adopting Secure Blockchain Practices

With the understanding of how blockchain works and its vulnerabilities, the adoption of specific proactive secure blockchain practices can help mitigate these risks. Let's explore some key practices.

1. Regular Updates: All devices involved in the blockchain network should be updated with the latest software patches. It helps in addressing any vulnerabilities that may occur.

2. Multi-Signature Wallets: For crypto-assets, consider a multi-signature wallet requiring more than one key to authorize a transaction. It adds an extra layer of protection against unauthorized transactions.

3. Wallet Backups: Regular backups of your crypto-wallets can ensure recovery of assets in case of device failures, loss, or theft.

4. Use of Hardware Wallets: These wallets store the user's private keys in a secure hardware device. It is the safest way to manage and trade cryptocurrencies.

7.3. Cybersecurity Measures for Blockchain

Specifically, from a cybersecurity perspective, the following measures add an additional layer of protection to your blockchain information.

1. Cold Storage: Cryptocurrencies can be stored offline, free from online vulnerabilities. Cold storage might involve storing information on hardware not connected to the internet or even paper wallets.

2. Two-factor authentication (2FA): It requires users to confirm their identity through a secondary device or method, reducing the risk of unauthorized access.

3. Regular Security Audits: Security audits are routine inspections of code and practices to identify any potential weaknesses or vulnerabilities.

4. Antivirus/Anti-malware solutions: Installing reliable antivirus or anti-malware solutions can increase protection against potential threats.

7.4. Educating Users about Blockchain Security

Finally, it's imperative that users who interact with blockchain technology understand the fundamentals of blockchain security. They should be aware of potential risks, how phishing or cyber attacks work, and how to detect and avoid them. They need to understand that the strength of their security largely depends on the security of their private keys, hence should never share them and always store them securely.

Educating users about secure blockchain practices and informing them of potential threats is a critical step towards securing blockchain information. It promotes safe and responsible dealings with digital assets, proving instrumental in preserving digital inheritance.

In conclusion, ensuring the security of blockchain information is a multi-tiered approach. It requires a thorough understanding and careful application of proactive secure blockchain practices, robust cybersecurity measures, and comprehensive user education. As more people immerse themselves in the realm of cryptocurrencies and digitized assets, ensuring the security of these assets becomes not only crucial but necessary in safeguarding the future of digital inheritance.

Chapter 8. Legal Landscape and Regulatory Challenges in Digital Inheritance

The legal standing of cryptocurrencies and other digital assets is always evolving and becoming more complex. As a new field, digital inheritance law is still very much underdeveloped and undefined. Today's inheritors and executors find themselves in a grey area, navigating often conflicting international laws and regulations.

8.1. Current Regulatory Status

The regulatory landscape of digital inheritance is experiencing growing recognition of the complexities involved in managing digital assets post-death. In many jurisdictions, however, there is no overarching regulation or policy guiding the inheritance process for crypto-assets. On the other hand, conventional assets are typically covered by clear legislation on estate and inheritance tax; this is less clear for cryptocurrencies and other digital assets.

For example, the U.S. Internal Revenue Service (IRS) treats digital assets, such as cryptocurrencies, as property for tax purposes. That means they're subject to federal property tax laws, which apply to inheritance. Transfers of digital assets by way of death are subject to the same estate taxation rules as other types of property, with the taxable value being the fair market value at the date of the decedent's death.

In the European Union, the situation is different. Even though the European Banking Authority has recommended applying anti-money laundering laws to cryptocurrency exchanges and custodial wallet providers, the regulation of crypto-assets in connection with inheritance law remains fragmented and inconsistent across the EU member states.

A few nations, such as Japan, Switzerland, and South Korea, have progressive laws and guidelines for crypto-assets and may serve as regulatory models for other countries in the future.

8.2. Regulatory Challenges

The regulatory landscape sees multiple difficulties with digital asset inheritance. This starts with identifying the assets and heirs, then proceeds with the transfer of ownership, and finally, ends with the taxation of those assets.

Cryptocurrencies, for instance, are kept in digital wallets secured by cryptography. Accessing these wallets requires a private key - a form of secret password. Should this password be lost or not provided to an inheritor, the wallet and its funds could forever remain inaccessible. Moreover, even when the private key is known, the anonymous nature of blockchain technology can make it challenging to determine an asset's owner.

Furthermore, the immutable and irrevocable nature of blockchain transactions can mean assets are directly transferred to an heir's wallet, bypassing the traditional probate process entirely. This direct transference can lead to problems, particularly where wills are contested or where a legal estate distribution framework is absent or ignored.

Complexities can also arise in the taxation of inherited digital assets. Given cryptocurrencies' volatile nature, the value of inherited digital assets can rapidly change, adding another layer of complexity to the taxing process.

8.3. The Need for Legal Frameworks

There is an urgent need for more comprehensive legal frameworks addressing the inheritance of digital assets. Many legal issues related to crypto-assets and blockchain technology, such as those involving contracts, securities, and taxes, could be decided by courts in the coming years. But for now, a lack of clear legal guidelines on digital inheritance issues often leaves individuals, families, and even legal professionals in the dark.

The starting point for this framework should be recognizing digital assets as a new category of property that can be inherited. To mitigate the risk of disputes concerning the allocation and taxation of digital assets, governments at the national and international levels need to integrate digital assets into existing legal systems and tax frameworks.

The framework should further include a clear process for digital asset inheritance, including detailed provisions on encryption, online security measures, and the legal rights of beneficiaries. It should codify proper digital estate planning practices, so crypto-asset holders can leave behind clear instructions for accessing and managing their digital wealth after their death.

8.4. Looking Forward

As more people invest in digital assets and build substantial holdings, the necessity of clear laws guiding digital inheritance becomes even more critical. We can expect a series of landmark court cases, legislative amendments, and regulatory guidelines emerging globally in the next decade, shedding light on this critical aspect in the laws of inheritance.

Some jurisdictions have already started to address this issue. For example, the Revised Uniform Fiduciary Access to Digital Assets Act

(RUFADAA) in the US has provided some clarity on how to manage digital assets, including access details, after the accountholder's death. However, more work needs to be done at a broader scale.

The legal and regulatory challenges involved in digital inheritance invite legal scholars, financial advisors, estate attorneys, and policy makers to probe this intersection of law and technology. Developing workable solutions will be crucial, ensuring the swift, effective transfer of digital assets and protecting the rights of all parties involved.

Chapter 9. Pitfalls to Avoid in Crypto Asset Protection

Entering the world of digital inheritance and crypto asset protection is similar to stepping into a dense forest with a complex web of roots and overgrown flora. Each step requires caution to avoid pitfalls and common errors that many individuals encounter on this journey. Whether you are an experienced investor with significant crypto wealth or a newcomer to this digital realm, it's crucial to navigate this space with care and comprehensive understanding of potential risks.

9.1. Not Recognizing the Value of Digital Assets

The first step in crypto asset protection is recognizing their monetary as well as data value. Many people, even those heavily invested in cryptocurrencies, tend to undervalue their assets, which in turn, leads to inadequate security measures. The statement "I don't have enough for it to matter" is a common fallacy. No matter the size of your crypto portfolio, it holds value that can grow exponentially over time. This underestimation often results in risky behavior like storing keys and passwords on open platforms, not backing up wallets, and relying too heavily on exchanges for storage.

9.2. Neglecting Long-Term Asset Security Measures

Failing to plan for long-term security is another common pitfall. Not all platforms or wallets will remain viable or safe indefinitely, and even the most secure storage solution can become a risk without regular updates and ongoing maintenance. In this constantly evolving technological landscape, relevant security measures must be reviewed and updated to match the pace.

Risk scenarios like losing access due to loss of a private key, forgetting passwords, or not having a record of ownership are potential consequences of neglecting long-term security. To overcome them, it's crucial to use security measures like a hardware wallet for storing your private keys and regularly back up your digital wallets. Moreover, up-to-date records of crypto transactions and ownership should be maintained.

9.3. Family or Heirs Not Being Aware of the Assets

Most people are adept at handling their digital assets while they're alive, but they often overlook one crucial aspect; making sure their loved ones are aware of their digital assets and can access them in the event of the asset owner's death.

Thus, creating a comprehensive inventory of digital assets, including cryptocurrencies, digital wallets, and exchange accounts, is paramount. This information, coupled with access instructions, should be kept in a secure location, and trusted family members or legal representatives should be made aware of its existence and storage location.

9.4. Lack of Legal and Estate Planning

Legal and estate planning is as critical for digital assets as it is for traditional assets. In many jurisdictions, crypto assets are not automatically passed on to heirs even if a will is in place. Instead, specific instructions need to be laid out in the estate plan. Without these, the court may not recognize the heirs' rightful claim to the digital assets. Consequently, instead of the assets being used as intended, they could eventually become inaccessible or even be deemed as unclaimed.

To prevent this, it's recommended to consult with legal professionals with experience in crypto matters. Planning should include the designation of beneficiaries, instructions related to the event of incapacity, tax instructions, and the inclusion of digital assets in a will or trust, if necessary.

9.5. Trusting Third Parties Implicitly

Crypto asset ownership is often inextricably linked with reliance on third parties like digital wallet providers or crypto exchanges. However, these third parties can be hacked, exit scam, or simply become insolvent. Trusting them implicitly puts your digital inheritance at risk.

Therefore, diversifying storage, maintaining local backups, and using multi-signature wallets where the private keys are spread amongst trusted parties can mitigate risks associated with third party platforms.

9.6. Neglecting Repercussions of Taxation

Finally, the implications of taxes on crypto assets cannot be neglected. Inheritance tax and country-specific cryptocurrency tax laws can come into play after the owner's death, thereby significantly impacting the asset value. Failing to consider these tax impacts can lead to a significant reduction in the inheritance's worth. Accordingly, understanding the tax jurisdiction's implications is a vital step towards effective planning for your crypto-assets.

In conclusion, avoiding these pitfalls can go a long way towards effective digital inheritance planning and crypto asset protection. Navigating this complex landscape requires meticulous planning, legal counsel, and a commitment to continuous education and awareness about the ever-evolving crypto space. By adopting these strategies, you can ensure your digital assets are preserved and passed on securely and efficiently.

Chapter 10. Future Trends and Developments in Digital Inheritance

The landscape of digital inheritance is developing and evolving rapidly, driven by the ongoing growth in the number of digital assets, particularly cryptocurrencies, and the increasing need to manage these assets after their owners' demise. To better comprehend this rising phenomenon, it's crucial to look at some future trends and developments that could shape the handling of digital inheritance.

10.1. Technological Innovations

Evidently, one of the critical factors affecting digital inheritance's future outlook is the underlying technology. Technological innovations, such as the implementation of smart contracts, can make the process of transferring digital assets after death more secure and efficient. These self-executing contracts can be programmed to automatically execute when specific conditions are met, such as upon confirmation of the owner's death.

Blockchain technology itself offers transparency, security, and efficiency, qualities that are critical in managing digital inheritance. Advancements in this technology can enhance the robustness of digital inheritance systems, making it almost impossible to tamper with the property rights or the transfer of assets. One such example is decentralized storage solutions which aim to provide safer and more reliable spaces for storing digital asset keys, thereby enhancing the security associated with digital inheritance.

10.2. Regulatory Changes

The absence of clear regulations around digital assets is a significant challenge hampering the streamlining of digital inheritance. Regulatory clarity is needed to ensure the legal transfer of digital assets after the owner's death, safeguarding these assets from theft and unauthorized access. Future regulations will likely recognize digital assets as the rightful property of the deceased, enabling heirs to inherit and manage these assets.

There's also an expectation that the future will see more cross-border regulations for digital assets. As digital assets transcend geographical boundaries, international law encounters challenges in managing digital inheritance, particularly when the deceased and the beneficiary reside in different jurisdictions.

10.3. Shift in Societal Attitudes

As society becomes more digital and technology-dependent, there's a positive shift in attitudes towards digital inheritance solutions. People are recognizing the need and the value associated with securing their digital assets after death, leading to a stark increase in the adoption of digital inheritance planning solutions.

In the future, it's expected that more people will show willingness to incorporate digital assets into their estate planning. This trend could be driven by the continued increase in awareness about digital inheritance and measures available to secure digital assets posthumely.

10.4. Enhanced Privacy and Security Measures

Security and data protection issues are a major concern in managing digital inheritance, given that it involves sensitive information and valuable assets. Future advancements in digital inheritance solutions will likely incorporate enhanced security features to guarantee data protection and privacy, alleviating potential risks associated with the transfer of digital assets after death.

Multi-factor authentication, encryption, secure key storage, and blockchain technology will continue to play vital roles in ensuring that only the rightful inheritors can access the digital assets.

10.5. Increased Cryptocurrency Adoption

The growing global adoption of cryptocurrencies lays the groundwork for a substantial increase in the importance of digital inheritance. According to recent surveys, the number of cryptocurrency users is skyrocketing each year, with a sizable percentage of the global population now owning digital currencies. Bitcoin, Ethereum, and other cryptocurrencies represent substantial value, and these currencies are often stored in digital wallets, which necessitates secure transmission protocols after the owner's demise.

As cryptocurrency adoption continues to surge, there's an increasing need for effective digital estate planning to ensure that these assets are not lost posthumously.

10.6. Role of Big Tech and Fintech

In the future, there's potential for greater involvement from Big Tech and Fintech companies in the realm of digital assets and, consequently, digital inheritance. Their entrance into the market can significantly shape the direction of digital inheritance planning, both from a structural and regulatory standpoint.

These companies have the technological expertise and the resources to develop advanced digital inheritance solutions, and they already manage a significant amount of user data. Giving users the option to plan their digital inheritance within these platforms can streamline the process, increasing convenience for users and enhancing the security of digital assets.

In conclusion, the realm of digital inheritance is gaining recognition as a pressing issue in today's digitally driven society. The future trends suggest a clear shift towards a secure, efficient, and legally recognized digital inheritance framework that ensures easy access to digital assets after their owners' demise. However, to reach this point, efforts must be made on both technological and regulatory fronts while making sure to prioritize privacy and security. Proper education and awareness are also vital so that more users, particularly the increasing number of cryptocurrency owners, are encouraged to consider digital inheritance planning seriously. This chapter merely scratches the surface of the potential advancements in digital inheritance - a topic that will continue to evolve with the digital world.

Chapter 11. Case Studies: Real-world Strategies for Digital Wealth Protection

The realm of digital inheritance presents a myriad of opportunities, but it's always insightful to learn from real life instances. In this chapter, we delve into some case studies that reveal the triumphs and trials of digital wealth protection.

11.1. Case Study 1: John's Forgotten Fortune

John was an early adopter of Bitcoin and amassed a considerable fortune. After a sudden and unexpected passing, his family came forward to claim his assets. However, they learned that only John had access to his private keys needed to unlock his Bitcoin wallet. The family was left bewildered and grief-stricken, staring at a lost fortune that could never be recovered.

This case serves as a stark warning about the importance of sharing information about digital assets - not necessarily the private keys or passwords, which could lead to misuse if fallen into the wrong hands, but at least information about their existence, storage location, and ways to access them. A trusted legal advisor can be of help to manage sensitive information securely and legally.

11.2. Case Study 2: Anna's Prepared Planning

In contrast is Anna, who owned a range of crypto assets. Understanding the digital inheritance implications, she used a decentralized application (DApp) to ensure her digital assets would be passed on efficiently. She set up a smart contract on Ethereum, which automatically transferred her assets to her kids' wallets upon her demise.

Anna's strategy demonstrates how technology can guarantee seamless and timely transfer of digital inheritance. However, using smart contracts and DApps like Anna requires a certain degree of technical know-how and understanding of the crypto ecosystem. It is suggested to take help of technologically equipped experts in this field, before proceeding with the setup.

11.3. Case Study 3: David's Trust-Based System

Another way to protect your digital assets is the approach that David took. He used a password manager to store his private keys and passwords, and trusted a legal representative with a master password. In the event of his death, the representative had a legal obligation to provide this master password to David's designated beneficiaries.

David's case epitomizes ease and security. However, trusting another party with sensitive information does present its own risks. To overcome this risk, it is advised to use a digitally signed and legally binding document that dictates the sharing of the master password in the event of an unforeseen circumstance.

11.4. Case Study 4: Emma's Vault Strategy

Emma pursued a more traditional approach to secure her crypto assets. She recorded her private keys and additional information on a piece of paper and stored it in a secured vault with instructions to her heirs about its location and importance. She also mentioned this in her will.

While Emma's strategy may not be feasible for everyone due to the physical nature of the process, it provides a straightforward method for those who are less technologically inclined. However, it is crucial to ensure the physical document's safety to prevent loss and theft.

To conclude, these case studies illustrate various methods for safeguarding digital assets after one's death. Different strategies can be more or less suitable depending on the individual's circumstances and technical expertise. The key takeaways are always to:

- Inform the trusted individuals about the existence of your digital assets.

- Make provisions for beneficiaries to access these assets.

- And, consider seeking professional advice to devise the most suitable method according to your personal circumstances.

Digital assets represent a new frontier in estate planning requiring unique strategies to ensure these valuable assets don't disappear into digital oblivion. Make sure you are planning properly and using the best tools and strategies at your disposal.